PRAISE FOR MACLAY'S TRANSFORMATIONS

"Jordan Maclay is a rare combination of scientist and poet. He is William Shatner blasting off on Jeff Bezos' rocket. The scientist in him studies the Universe in his poems. He ponders the possibility of using gravity to power spaceships. The poet in him ponders the hoard of damp boxes in his basement, the residue of seventy-plus years of living. He worries about taxes. He loves his old dog. He is afraid to dive deep into his pond - he fears the darkness. He fails at love. He washes away his sins in the shower. I love the book; it is so personal. His poems are confessional. They are for Everyman and Everywoman. I loved the drawings, so colorful and quirky, they are necessary. It makes it more of a surprise when you turn the page."

-ELLIS FELKER, POET, RED OAK PUBLISHERS, AUTHOR OF "MOLAKAI DREAMS," "BOAZ MOON," AND NUMEROUS OTHER POETRY BOOKS.

"In this charming little volume, Jordan touches us deeply by sharing the inner workings of his heart and soul."

-CARVER MEAD, PH.D., GORDON, AND BETTY MOORE EMERITUS PROFESSOR OF ENGINEERING AND APPLIED SCIENCE, CALIFORNIA INSTITUTE OF TECHNOLOGY, NATIONAL MEDAL OF TECHNOLOGY, INVENTORS HALL OF FAME, AUTHOR OF "COLLECTIVE ELECTRODYNAMICS: QUANTUM FOUNDATIONS OF ELECTROMAGNETISM," "INTRODUCTION TO VLSI SYSTEMS," AND "ANALOG VLSI AND NEURAL SYSTEMS."

"I have known Dr. Maclay for 40 years now, as a fellow entrepreneur and dear friend. Jordan is a lover of life and he dares to dive deeply into its mysteries. He is a world-class intellect yet

his passionate love of art and beauty is a wonderful balance to his mental acuity. This shows up clearly in this book of poetry and art; what a gift to all of us this book is!"

-DAVID K. BANNER, PH.D., EMERITUS PROFESSOR OF MANAGEMENT, WALDEN UNIVERSITY, AUTHOR OF "*LOVING IT ALL, LIVING WITH AN AWAKING HEART*," "*FRAME SHIFTING: A PATH TO WHOLENESS*," AND "*DESIGNING EFFECTIVE ORGANIZATIONS: TRADITIONAL AND TRANSFORMATIONAL VIEWS*."

"Transformations truly evokes the soul of life experiences; it relates to the wonders and enigma of living a human life; very expressive and provocative; thoughtful."

-JOSEPH R. STETTER, PH.D., ENTREPRENEUR, PRESIDENT OF SPEC-SENSORS, LLC AND KWJ ENGINEERING INCORPORATED

"Reading Jordan Maclay's Transformations, a series of essays, poems, and drawings, quite beautiful, a gem, I was captured by his easy give and take from the magical mystical to the scientific and philosophical. The interplay is between his personal connection with the intricate folds of a mind exploring the Mystery. He offers personal declarations of love with such open vulnerability. He offers us playful, magical drawing that reminds me of a mixture of John Lennon and Paul Klee. His training as a physicist/researcher is tinged with his lifelong quest and introspection in meditation and mysticism.

What is evident over and over is his vulnerability. In his poem, "Do I Dare" he questions the courage, his own courage to reveal "Who I am." He declares "throw off my shield" and reveal myself, "like a butterfly escaping from its chrysalis." This work continues to reveal the great penetration by the wise scientist/explorer/lover of life and reveals all that he has touched and been touched by in life. As we read the multiple poems and self-disclosures we *discover a Modern Renaissance Man, with comically poetic mysticism and a penetrating intellect. Dr. Maclay oscillates between the Cosmic Mystic in the "Dance of Science" and the earthly pragmatist, ruminating on his decision to spend $3060.30 in his "Home Theater-Stereo" piece. His openness and honesty again are affirmed in his "Epilog," where he writes of his "carefully constructed inferiority complex," being mediated by his "Spirit [which] watches amused at all my gyrations, quietly loving me."*

-NORMAN ANDREKUS, PH.D., LICENSED PSYCHOLOGIST

"Jordan Maclay has had a lifelong passion for scientific, artistic, and spiritual exploration. This unusual book is mainly a collection of short poems and other material relating to his quest for meaning, purpose, and self-fulfillment in these explorations. While serious and deeply personal, it is presented with a sense of humor and compassion, and will likely be appreciated and enjoyed especially by like-minded readers pondering their own 'transformations.'"

-PETER W. MILONNI, PH.D., LABORATORY FELLOW AT LOS ALAMOS NATIONAL LABORATORY, RESEARCH PROFESSOR AT UNIVERSITY OF ROCHESTER, NY, AUTHOR OF "THE QUANTUM VACUUM," "LASER PHYSICS," AND "AN INTRODUCTION TO QUANTUM OPTICS AND QUANTUM FLUCTUATIONS."

*"Some years ago, Jordan Maclay came to my office at the University of Washington and introduced himself, expressing an interest in my work on the interpretation of quantum mechanics. That was the beginning of a series of very productive interactions. In the most recent of those, he solicited and edited a long paper published in the journal **Symmetry**, in which Carver Mead and I described for the first time the intrinsic mechanism behind*

quantum wave function collapse. Without Jordan, that paper would never have been written.

In all the years of interacting with Jordan, I had no idea that he was a poet and artist, and that in the course of his work in physics he would be inspired to place poems and pictures among his technical notes. This book, containing that work, reveals a whole new aspect of his character that I had not even suspected. But now, in this small volume, we have the evidence, a collection of his poems and art.

When he described the book to me, I was expecting that it would reflect his work as a scientist, exploring aspects of quantum phenomena. There is some of this in the book, but most of the poems reflect Jordan, the human being rather than Jordan, the scientist. I find that refreshing and enlightening. I hope you do too."

-JOHN G. CRAMER, PH.D., PROFESSOR EMERITUS UNIVERSITY OF WASHINGTON, AUTHOR OF "THE QUANTUM HANDSHAKE: ENTANGLEMENT, NONLOCALITY AND TRANSACTIONS," "EINSTEIN'S BRIDGE", AND "TWISTOR."

TRANSFORMATIONS

Poetry And Art

G. Jordan Maclay, PhD

Published by
Quantum Fields LLC

www.quantumfields.com

Library of Congress Control Number: **2021925391**

International Standard Book Number: 978-0-578-34483-6

www.gjordanmaclay.com

To Mary,

whose unconditional love and support have been

the greatest blessing of my life.

ACKNOWLEDGMENTS

This book would not have been possible without the collaboration of Mary, my wife of over 35 years, who can do anything.

For their inspiration and support I thank my collaborators and friends, Marc Millis of NASA, Dr. Peter Milonni, Dr. Joseph Stetter, Professor John G. Cramer, Professor Garret Moddel, Dr. Eric Davis, Dr. Hal Puthoff, Dr. David K. Banner, Diane Banner, Moody Ahmad, Reba Ahmad, Gordon Glass, Ellis Felker, Valerie Mangion, John Fergus, Deb Schwarz, Laura Berger, John Stauber, Danny Turner, Marty Clearfield, Dr. Norman Andrekus, Professor Hal Fearn, Henk Neuenhaus, Linda Gentes, and Michael Fardad Serry. To my brother Otis Maclay for his support and good humor.

I especially thank my children, Colin, Mona, and Matthew Maclay for their love and inspiration and for how much I have learned from them.

Author's Preface

"Transformations" explores the challenges that I faced at a critical time in my life, and that many of us may face. Are we enough? Are we honest with ourselves? Are we true to ourselves and to others? The poems and art explore, with humor and compassion, the transformations I experienced moving beyond the challenges into the light and freedom of self-expression and self-fulfillment.

There is another meaning to the word "transformation," a technical meaning from quantum physics. To determine the essential properties of an object, we can look at the same object in a transformed coordinate system, which means at different locations, at different times, moving at different velocities.

Whatever properties remain the same during this transformation represent the essence of the object. For elementary particles, it is the mass and the spin. For people, I believe it is the spirit or the soul: at the core, we are spirit experiencing our space-time world of human activities. I experienced this perspective and it is expressed in several poems.

The poems and art reflect what were my everyday personal challenges and victories: being present, being loving, taking risks, expressing doubts, showing determination, engaging in self-reflection, observing the mind and the shadow side, creating renewal, acknowledging death and the divine within us.

Some of the poems describe the joy and challenges I felt leaving my tenured university position and moving to the country with my wife, our two young children, and our two dogs. Some of the poems reflect the overwhelming technical issues I faced working on exciting and revolutionary programs in quantum physics for NASA, exploring the use of quantum energy in empty space to propel rockets, and the use of entanglement to establish a communication link with no broadcast power and with no limitation on distance.

Two additional catalysts for my transformation were my becoming a Black Belt in Shaolin Kempo Karate and a Master Practitioner in Neuro-Linguistics Programming (NLP).

The mixed-media drawings were done with oil pastels, watercolors, art markers, and ink. The metal sculpture is welded steel. The poems and art were created independently of each other.

TABLE OF CONTENTS

WHO

I don't mean to be impertinent but

DO YOU KNOW WHO YOU ARE?
Do you recognize your voice?
Do you know your smell?
The touch of your index finger?

Would you recognize yourself from the back?
Would you know yourself in the dark?
Do you know How you make decisions?

I don't mean to be impertinent but
Does a fish know about the water?
Does a painter KNOW a blank canvas?

What is your reflection in a blank mirror without silver?
Even your obituary won't tell.

The secret is in the illusion.
Brilliant Light from the sun
from the stars
is focused in a spot.
We watch this spot this insignificant spot
so carefully, so very, very carefully
and forget the sun, the stars, the heavens.

The smell of wet fur, a warning.
A tiger's claw
pierces the flesh,
a drop of blood
leaks from the torn skin.
A sigh is heard.
Time for bactine
Time for triple antibiotic ointment
mercurochrome and
hydrogen peroxide,
zinc oxide and calamine,
benzocaine and bozocaine,
valium and viagra,
tylenol and tampax,
to save us from ourselves

BOXES IN THE BASEMENT

When I review my life,
reading the old diaries
My heart wobbles,
my breath becomes shallow as the struggles
reappear

But That is like today my mind protests.
Or I have conquered that
my mind retorts.

My handwriting is unchanged.
So is my weight and height, my old resume says.

The cornerstones of achievement folded neatly,
have begun to disintegrate.

Is this me?
How could I have been so cruel? so thoughtless?

I will keep the evidence buried in the basement,
or in the folds of my cortex.

Will I be "over" in 70 years, like the rain?
or "done", like a muffin?

Am I my past, my future, or
The present?

DO I DARE

Do I dare be who I am?
A question I asked myself 20 years ago.
Did I?
Was I me?
Am I a process continually changing and
developing and refining
itself?
OR do I just never really change?

I am scared.

Maybe I won't do anything good.
I will just screw around and
do bits and pieces,
never having the courage to reveal who I am.

It's my choice.

At Last, Yogi Peponi's Program For Enlightenment

If you truly accept something about yourself
then you can change.
Of course, the fear is that if you deeply accept something
about yourself
then it will never change.

To change, you must face and accept your greatest fears.
To accept your fears, you must face your face, without fear
of fear, or fear of losing face.

The face of fear is to fear that fear itself cannot be faced
without deep fear. Indeed, to be perfectly clear,
life is like a face, like a pizza: round, cooked, and divided
into slices that are consumed in several bites.

You eat it; it does not eat you.
You take home whatever is left over,
and you eat it for breakfast the next day.
Every day, be sure to eat something meaningful.

TYRANNY OF HISTORY

I looked through the musty boxes. Some of the papers were brown and fragile (from the high acid content of the inexpensive paper). Mice had eaten edges of the newspapers. I found a box of old resumes, from the half pager in high school, to the 12 pages "complete" C.V. The files on checks started in 1962, from freshman year in college, then to the accounts in Virginia, New York, Connecticut, Illinois, and Vermont. The wooden boxes of old tools were harder to open. The brass oxy-acetylene torches were tarnished and covered with dust. The clothes provided a historical interlude. What was once so fashionable now is awkward and irrelevant. Homework and school papers, with comments in red, from forgotten courses, unseen since they were so carefully packed, living monuments to effort. Room after room, piled to the ceiling: rent receipts, shopping bags, National Geographics, 78 records, medical receipts, report cards, drivers licenses, letters, travel documents, photographs, underpants, calendars, notes from ex-wives, graduate admission letters, sketches, security deposit agreements, employment offers, airplane ticket receipts, eyeglasses, buttons, and God knows what else. The floors sagged under the weight. Truly a monument to struggle, to death.

Without a doubt, one of the greatest gifts is forgetfulness, God loosening the chains of the past. Otherwise, we slowly expire, crushed by the baggage.

HERE

My life flows by
While I watch
The ripples of my struggle
Disappear

And although
The seasons change
I remain always
Here

12

THE BIG BANG

When I open my eyes,
The dawn comes,
A new world is born.

When I am sick,
When a bee is floating in the water struggling to be free,
life struggles.

When I smile,
When I laugh,
A cascade of love flows through the canyons.

When I doubt,
Darkness spreads,
Music becomes a cacophony,
And I am alone.

When I love,
Light fills the universe,
Flowers bloom, birds sing.

When I put my face against my horse's soft coat,
When I smell him,
I am roaming the plains between the stars.

When I feel my wife's soft, warm body,
I am embraced and the world is protected.

When I close my eyes,
The universe goes to sleep and is forgotten.

Friday, October 19, 2007, 5:10 AM

UNITY

I want to be laughing more
I need to be crying more
I want to be loved more
I need to be more loving
If all is the sum of its parts
I am part of it all
I part with it all
And celebrate my unity with the universe

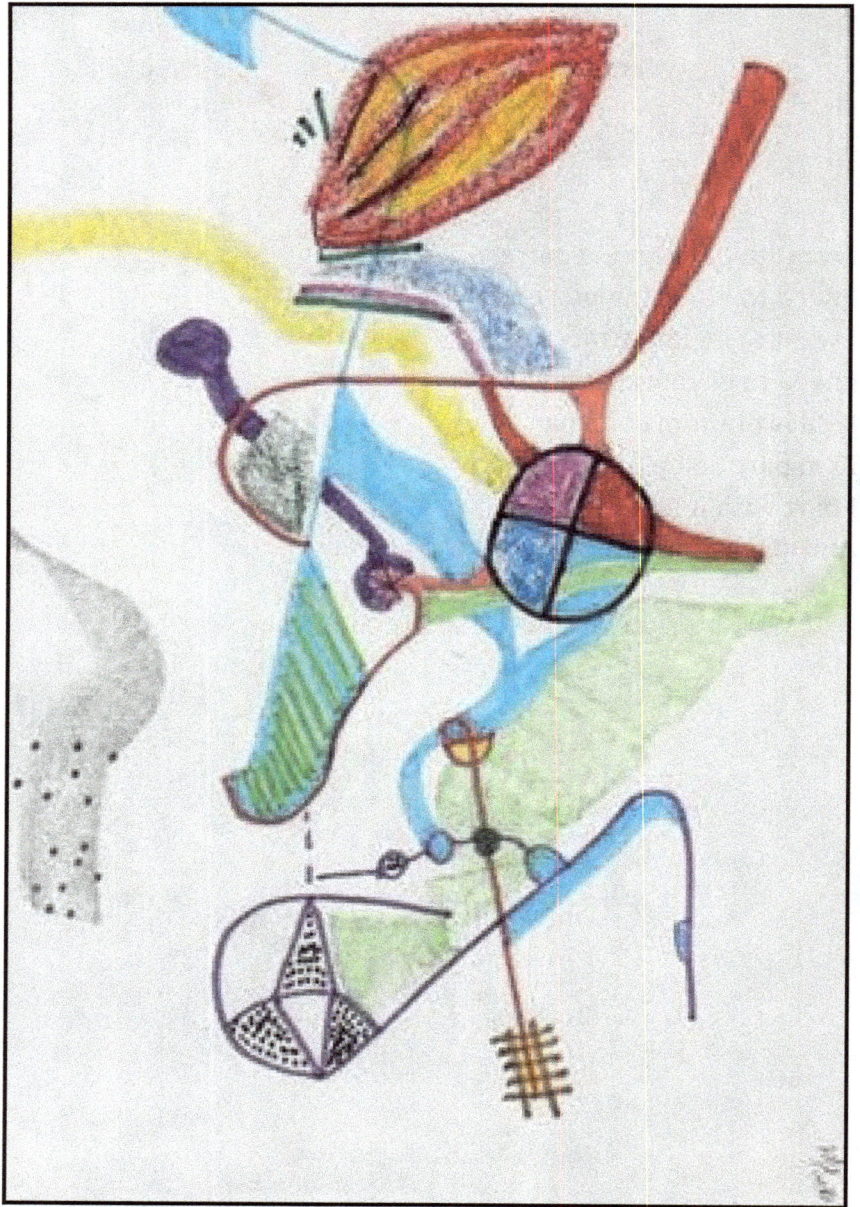

COURAGE

Inside
a cocoon
so comfortable
nestled in a prophylactic
womb
I wait
and watch hidden
facets of myself
reflected in the
creations of warriors
while I corrode.

The pain
sparks me to BE
I fling off my shield and
reveal myself
I fly

THE SUN SHINES

I stood in front of a mirror
With my seven-year-old son, Matthew.
He made a sad face.
I made a happy face.
He made a happy face.
I made a sad face.
He made a silly face.
I made a sillier face.
We laughed and made faces, scary faces,
Frog faces, sweet faces,
Dumb faces, pirate faces, right faces, left faces,
Even about faces,
Creating a wondrous world of joy and discovery
Alive in the mirror and in our eyes.

It's nice to know we can make so many faces.
It's nice to know I can have
Such a good time without batteries
Or the Internet.
My son calls it the joy of having a kid.

THE FLOOD AND THE BAPTISM

Every night I wash away the sins
the weaknesses, the failures to hit the target
that crippled me that day

With hot water
They go down the drain
with a sweet gurgle
effortlessly

I am baptized anew
I am a new being
Ready for a new world
And its challenges
Tomorrow.

ALIVE

I became as a small child,
alive to the subtle nuances of the
shades of grey, the footsteps of centipedes
the bright sun making crosses and stars in my eyes.

Suddenly it is so peaceful
so beautiful
the birds singing, the breeze and trees
so perfect forever, stillness
the inaudible echo of each sound projected into infinity.

Time has stopped for me
in this perfect place and yes
this is my life I did not notice yesterday.

I recognize the dirt that
today is part of the completeness of perfection.
I smile and know it is no different than it was yesterday
when I was bored and tired.

TIME ON MY HANDS

Time on My Hands
Time on My Mind

I have time.
I don't have to do anything.
I can just sit
or do something else.
I have time to sit
time for visions
and revisions.

Usually, I don't have time to sit
or to read a book
or to watch a cloud
or to plant a daisy
or watch a star.

I work I work and I work
I work and I work I work
I wok and I wok and I rok
I wurk and wurk and I ruk
and I don't watch stars
and I don't listen to spring peepers.

Now I have time
I can smell the pine trees
and feel the breeze.

I can do anything but
I don't know what to do.
Who will schedule me and why and how?
How will I choose?

Do We Have To Get Older?

If there was no such thing as time, there would be no aging. Why do we have time? The answer, from a spiritual viewpoint, is that time forces us to grow, to sift the wheat from the chaff in our lives so that ultimately, both we and the cosmic forces hope we do the things that are important for us in life (for a discussion see "The Course in Miracles"). Without time, we would perennially act as youth does, with the sense of invulnerability, with unlimited time to accomplish whatever we want. But with the clock ticking, we must get to what is important. Or we will never get it done.

For some people, the most important thing is family life, sharing their children's lives, taking care of grandchildren. For others, it is their relationships with friends and relatives. For others, it is enjoying the moment. For others, it may be a professional accomplishment. Or it may be a mixture of things, as it is for me. But without time, I am not sure that we would converge on what is important. And even with time, some people fail to embrace that which is most important to them before they die. Let me give an example.

One of our most important relationships is that with our parents. For some, this relationship may be comfortable and easy, for others it may be very difficult and without evident mutual caring. For probably all of us, this relationship is of primary importance and is fundamental to our place (and our peace) in the world. One of the most important messages in life is the declaration of love between parent and child, and I don't mean, "She knows that I love her, even if I don't say it." I mean an overt declaration of love when one actually says the love and is sure that the other has heard it and knows that love is the bond between them.

For most of us, this declaration of love is fundamental to our well-being. Why do we sometimes wait until death is imminent to make this declaration of love? We all may have our "reasons" but it is always a relief if the declaration is finally made. The rivers of life may then flow freely.

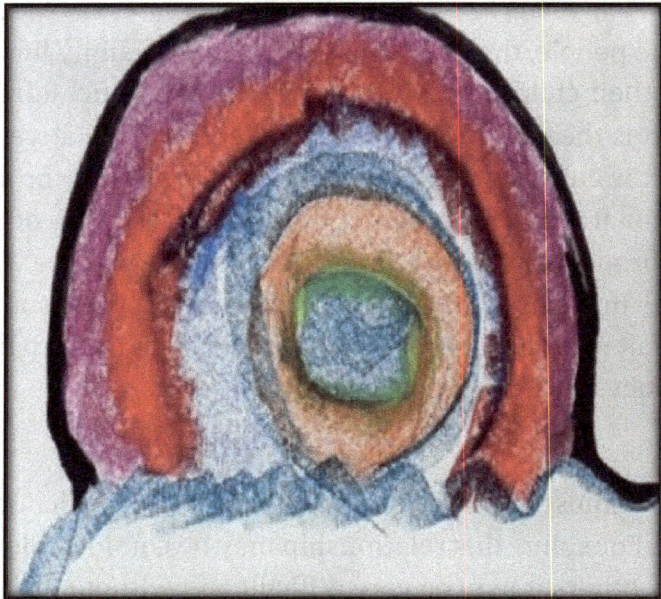

THE FOLLOWING

To follow is to surrender
my feelings, my needs, my thoughts, my personality
and cast them into the flames of the cosmic incinerator
leaving me naked
clothed in the garments of the birds of the air
and the lilies of the field.

To follow is to tumble
into the darkness
and trust.

To follow is to gaze at the fears in my mind
and walk on the dew-covered grass
when there is no sun or moon and
I can hear the owls
asking who cooks for you.

To follow is to leap into the dark pond and
risk being eaten by the monsters.

To follow is to be free
and hitch my chariot to the gods,
to rip off my cover
and fearlessly let

My light blaze
hoping
I am not struck down
by those who are offended.

I WAKE AT 2:17 AM

I wake at 2:17 AM.
Ideas of space travel filling my mind.

Like a Native American going into battle
I walk naked on the grass
In the moonlight

Up the hill to my office
And put the ideas on paper.

Like sailing with a gravity shield,
We can use gravity tacking to get to the stars.

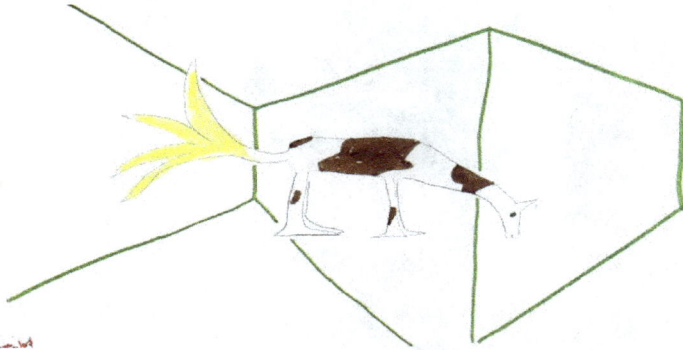

TRIPPING ON MY EGO

I am clumsy.
I am a clod.
I weave a cloud of
dreams I want to be,
a nest of invisible threads,
illusions to protect Me,
illusions to attack You.
The threads thicken into ropes
to bind and prove my worth and
then I cannot escape
the safety of my hell.

IN HI BITION

Fre eze
dri ed
love
Cho king
on a bad
id ea

Fear
feel ings
to take no risks
to risk no in ti mate images
to imagine no in ti ma cy that might shatter
a mir ror of personal pro wess.

Lu de ong
Lau de gaptus
Saucer Igator
Dowenascus.

To have lived not at all,
To have never stepped on an ant,
or risked the appearance of a
pterodactyl craning its folds
in a small glass jar
making no waves
isolated by fear
sealed tightly
without air.

BREAKDOWN

Little Tommy Turtle
Sitting on a Myrtle
Gasped for air
While passing gas

Slobbering sloths
With silver saliva in the moonlight
Are so sweet
Like honey on my feet.

Make friends with a fly.
Get to know a fly.
Share a meal with a fly.
They really aren't so bad.

Do something else
Do something you can't do
But do something you don't know you can't do
And just to prove it, do it well.

GOOSE BUMPS

Run your finger along with the razor, lightly,
Sit on the edge, listening
Reveal the inner tapestry, its transcendental beauty, and its
Grossness.

Goosebumps and the sound of one shoe falling.
Bite off more than you can chew
And then chew it.

THE TARANTULA

Furry striped arms that insinuate
a gravel tongue,
an abdomen throwing needles
to attack
and defend the fat fortress.

Tarantula - Orange peel

Darkness falls
the choice was made
and all that matters is gone.

All that is protected is nothing.

Can a fly be very sad?
I can.

Can a fly be very simple?
I can.

My little rabbit has soft fur and likes to play.
My little rabbit likes me to rub its face.
My little rabbit loves me.

I love my little rabbit.

QUANTUM QUESTIONS

I dip my ladle into the clear, flowing stream
my head thrown back
and drink deeply
the cool water
filling my mouth and throat.

I notice the deep waters.
I lean over to look into the dark waters.

Cautiously I lower my silver ladle
deep into the dark waters
deep into the black see
and watch it
and watch my hand, my arm disappear
into the darkness of the cold waters

A lone trembling child, fearful
poised to drown in
the mysterious waters
incomprehensibly trusting
with my throat on the block
trusting in surrender
to receive
the incomprehensible renewal of life.

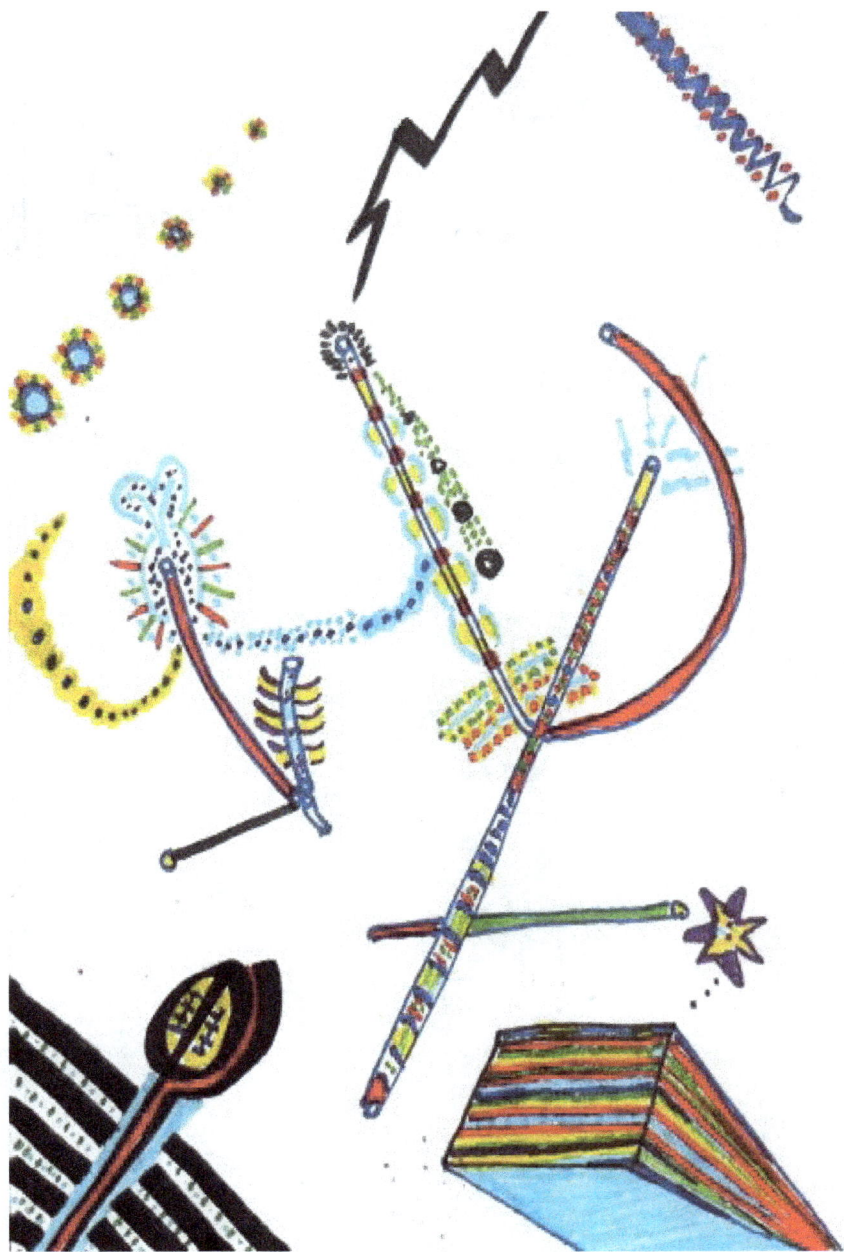

when $x = 0$

$$\hbar \omega'(0) = \hbar \omega_0 + \frac{\hbar \omega'(0)}{c^2} \frac{G}{2} \left(M - \frac{\hbar \omega_0}{c^2} \right) \frac{1}{L+\delta} + \frac{G\hbar}{}$$

$$\frac{\hbar \omega'(0)}{c^2} \frac{G}{2} \frac{M}{\delta}$$

when $x = L$ we had

$$\hbar \omega'(L) = \hbar \omega_0 + \frac{\hbar \omega'(L)}{c^2} \frac{G}{2} \left(M - \frac{\hbar \omega_0}{c^2} \right) \frac{1}{\delta} + \frac{\hbar \omega'(L)}{c^2} \frac{G}{2} \frac{M}{L+\delta}$$

By definition we will say $\omega'(L) = \omega_0$ (???)

$$\hbar \omega_0 = \hbar \omega'(L) \left[1 - \frac{G}{2c^2} \left(M - \frac{\hbar \omega_0}{c^2} \right) \frac{1}{\delta} - \frac{G}{2c^2} \frac{M}{L+\delta} \right]$$

$L \gg \delta$ so

$$\hbar \omega_0 \cong \hbar \omega'(L) \left[1 - \frac{G}{2c^2} \left(M - \frac{\hbar \omega_0}{c^2} \right) \frac{1}{\delta} \right] \qquad \left(\text{assumes } Mc^2 \gg \hbar \omega_0 \right)$$

At the open end

$$\hbar \omega_0 = \hbar \omega'(0) \left[1 - \frac{G}{2c^2} \left(M - \frac{\hbar \omega_0}{c^2} \right) \frac{1}{L+\delta} - \frac{G}{2c^2} \frac{M}{\delta} \right]$$

$$\hbar \omega_p \cong \hbar \omega_0'(0) \left[1 - \frac{G}{2c^2} \frac{M}{\delta} \right]$$

$$\therefore \hbar \omega_0'(L) \left[1 - \frac{G}{2c^2} \left(M - \frac{\hbar \omega_0}{c^2} \right) \frac{1}{\delta} \right] = \hbar \omega_0'(0) \left[1 - \frac{GM}{2c^2 \delta} \right]$$

$$\omega_0'(L) = \omega_0'(0) \frac{\left[1 - \frac{GM}{2c^2 \delta} \right]}{\left[1 - \frac{G}{2c^2} \left(M - \frac{\hbar \omega_0}{c^2} \right) \frac{1}{\delta} \right]}$$

$$= \omega_0'(0) \left(\frac{1-A}{1-A+B} \right) = \omega_0'(0) \frac{1}{1 + \frac{B}{1-A}}$$

$$\left(\text{note: diverges for } \delta \to 0 \right)$$

$$\omega_0'(L) = \omega_0'(0) \frac{1}{1 + \frac{G}{2c^2} \frac{\hbar \omega_0}{c^2} \frac{1}{\delta} \cdot \frac{1}{1 - \frac{GM}{2c^2} \frac{1}{\delta}}}$$

$$\omega_0'(L) \left(1 - \frac{G}{}\frac{\hbar \omega_0}{}\frac{1}{\delta} \right)$$

Random page from research journal - Gravitational effects on photons

RESEARCH

The fragile bones of knowledge
Deep in my hippocampus
I grope to feel their shapes
In the darkness.

From within, the light shines
Leading the way
Dimly sometimes
But always forward.

Energy in space
Space in energy
We are energy
We are space.

We are the field of all possibilities.

NOTES FROM BELOW

My secret friend
I court you

patiently
like a lover.

Listening for your presence
in the dark of my being.

Looking for the sweet sound
the small movement
the sweet smell.

You the dreamer
You have blessed me with the unknown
more than I know.

Come to me
My shy lover
who loves me
more than I know.

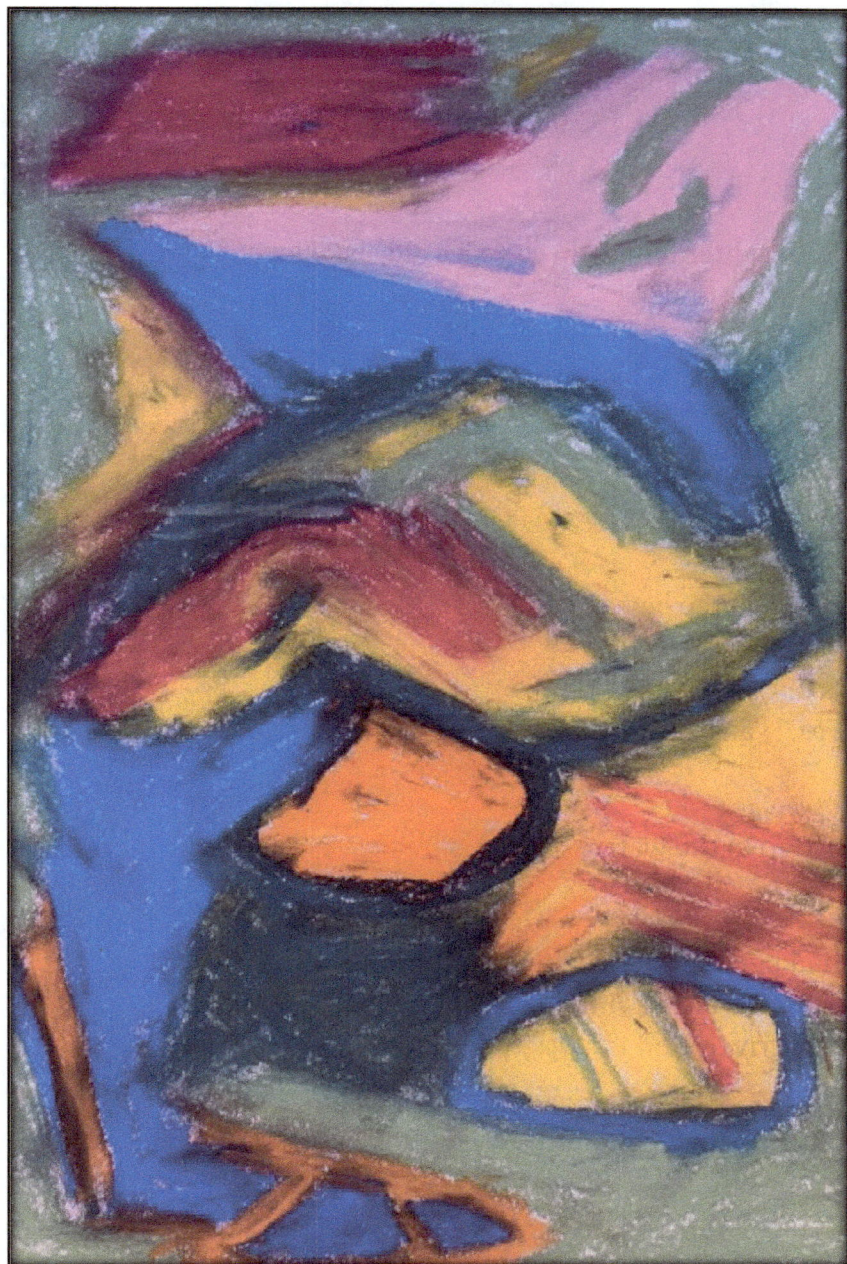

WHERE IS GOD?

My daughter Mona, three years old, asked me:
"Where is God?"

"Everywhere," I said. It was an easy question,
that I answered
automatically.

"Is God in the beaver?"
"Yes," I answered.
"Is God in the fox?"
"Yes," I answered.

"Is God in the water?"

I had been thinking of God as spirit.
There is a chant, "In the forest God is green;
In the river, God is restless."

"Yes, God is in water,"
I answered, thinking that I drink God
when I drink water,
which was a nice thought
that I had never had before.
"Is God in the Queen's Anne Lace?"
"Yes," I said, thinking how masters
talk of God peeking through the
infinite to us through the beauty of flowers.

"Is God in plastic?"
"Yes," I answered, reflecting that although
I don't like plastic much as a material,
it wouldn't make sense for
plastic to be an exception,
so God must be in plastic.

"Is there somewhere God isn't?"
"No, God is everywhere."

I remembered a story about three men who wanted to
be disciples of a great, wise saint. He told them each to
take a piece of fruit and eat it where no one could ever
know he was eating it. One ate it in a closet, another
ate it in a secluded meadow, and the third, who went to
dark caves, remote thickly wooded forests, and many
other secluded places, but could find no place so secret
that God was not there watching him eat the fruit.

Finally, he brought the banana back to the saint and became
his disciple.

Later that day we were in the bathroom, and as Mona
looked around the room, she asked me questions:

"Is God in the trash?"
I had never thought about this before but
by now I knew what the answer had to be:
"Yes."

"Is God in paper?"
"Yes."

"Is God in my bm?"

Again, Mona was teaching what it really means for God
to be everywhere. She already knew the answer.
"Yes."

I felt exhilarated and spread my arms,
feeling that God was really everywhere and in everything,
and that I was in God.
Mona asked me if God was in my arms, and I said
"Yes"

She asks without guile or attachment.
She demonstrates how to approach God, as a child.
We can learn so much from children.

A few days later Mona was asking about love.
I told Mona that God was love.
The love that I felt for her and
the love she felt for me or for her mom or grandmother
was God in her.
I told her God would not be complete without her.
Mona asked me if God loved her, yes, I replied.
Did God love a mouse, yes, a rabbit, yes.
Then she said:
"Does God love a murderer?"

As usual, she was getting to the heart of the issue. I was
unaware she even knew this word.
I thought of the story of the prodigal son.
"Yes, God loves a murderer."

Why do people have guns?"
"Because they are afraid someone may hurt them."

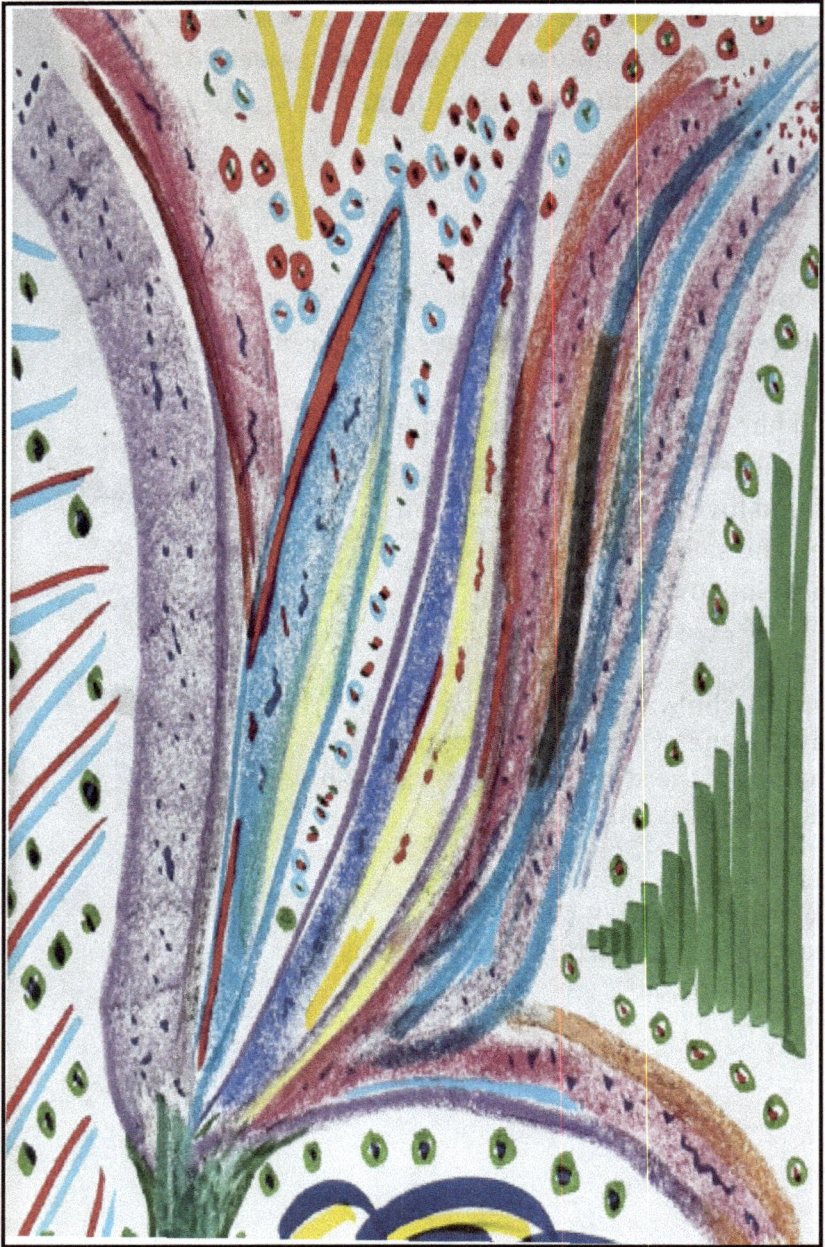

50

VERTEBRA

my mind replaces the energy of time
with my love
my body straining
to be free
to stretch my back in ways
it does not know
awakening each vertebra
to move into spaces
it does not know
to see myself
with my eyes
to free myself from my insides

DEAR BABY

Dear baby
I love you, baby, I hope you know
Ido ido ido ido

I love you baby, baby, I hope you know I do
so come on baby lets here to loving you.

Sometimes I am sorry I cannot be
More of what you want me to be
Sometimes it hurts to think that's so

Sometimes I wonder
What our purpose together is
Is it our vows
Is it really to merge
together in God

Sometimes I struggle
to express myself
And my love for you
I struggle to shed
those barriers and inhibitions

I cry for your love
I wish I could offer you more
All that I am I give to you

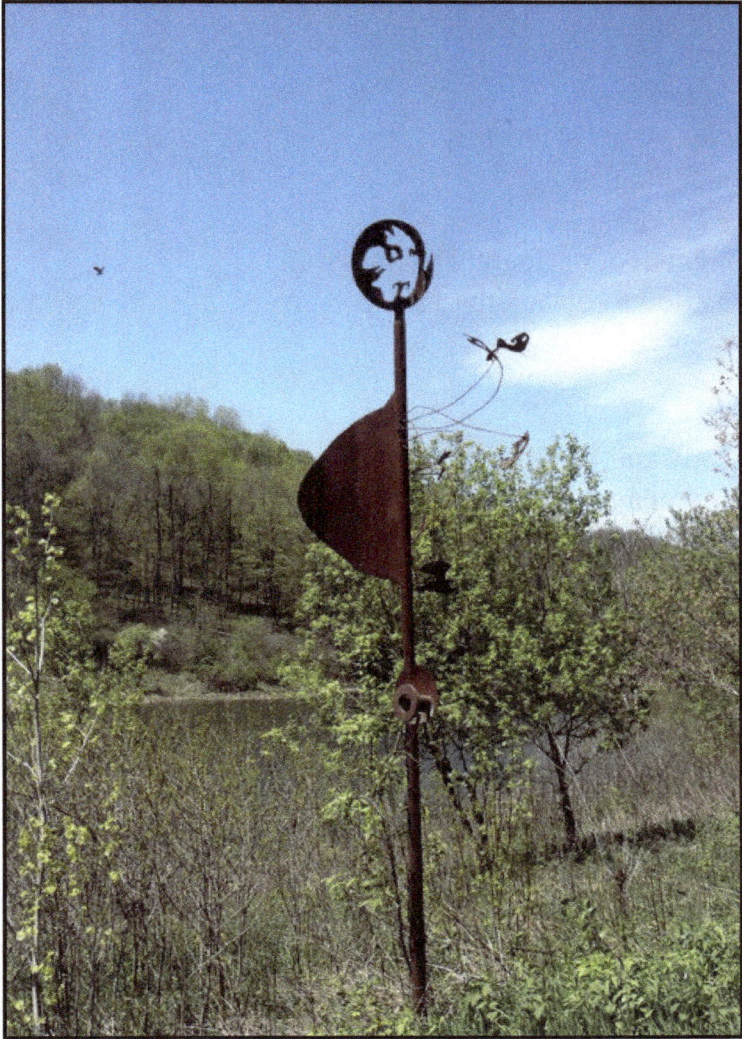

Pond Goddess, welded steel 12' x 4'

MY WAY

My way
The golden way
Lit by the lamps of eternity
With smoking oil
On my hands
The pungent odor floating by my side
Settling down curling up to sleep

My way
Is my way and I want you
To want my way to be your way

Walking by my side by your side
We gaze forward
Squinting
Asking for guidance
On our way

Secretly
I want you to want my way
But I will wait
And we will want together

WAKE UP TIME

The bell rings
Conditioned parts wake and salivate
Little red numbers on little red LEDs organize us.
Other parts sleep in so many ways
In so many places,
Under rocks and in claustrophobic corridors.
Is my elbow asleep or my nose?

Who knows when the ice melts,
And the water flows.
Forgotten buds turn green in the warm sunshine
That has traveled 150 million kilometers thru space
To remind us we need light
And love warmth.

Can a hand support a bud's growth,
Caressing it gently like the wind
As clouds disappear in the sky?

Some gardeners talk to their plants
And tell them of their loves and longings
Touching the heart with dew.

29,000 Feet Above Lake Michigan

This is the time one sees how fragile life is
hanging by a tenuous thread
the invisible divine support of a 188,679-pound bus
floating in the air
5.12 miles above a lake 613 feet deep
no strings
no safety nets
no mirrors.
my body feels so fragile
I feel the emptiness in my stomach
a mild tension
a waiting for the dominant chord,
bordering on pain
acknowledging what my eyes see out the window.
I always get a window seat.
(The balance is as delicate as natures ecology.)

What if the pneumatic system malfunctions
What if a stress crack develops
in the horizontal stabilizer
What if rotor blade number 216
in the engine turbine number 1
cracks after 127 billion rotations

or another of the 7 million parts breaks.
(Yes, and what if we kill all the mosquitoes?
What happens then?)
Does our fate depends on a million 3-dollar parts?

Floating above the lake,
I know this is the way
it always is
Always floating on the edge of life
tenuous.
It's not the things we see of the eyes
that keep us alive
It's not the things we make of our hands
that keep us alive
or kill us.
What we do not see with our eyes is what we are

What we do not see with our eyes is what
Fills us and fulfills
and keeps us floating
Above pain and suffering
Nestled in the infinite bosom of divine love

Vision is of the heart
Looking out of that window I see
God is love and therefore so am I.

In The Air

My body panics
My mind convinces it to not go berserk
Even though it is floating 5 miles above Lake Michigan
My spirit, like a guest who does not speak much,
Sits quietly, unworried, and just is.

BONES

Life flows into my cells
vibrating, glowing

The power to create
is mine
God given

I choose my work
until my time
ends

Flesh decays
into gases, that someone
breathes and
into bones we make
clubs and ladles from.

What remains
cannot be seen
and never could

Yet it is always there

RHYTHMS

Circadian rhythms
my pulse
my breath
the period of my pendula:
my legs, my arms
my cilia

The tension/relaxation cycle of my muscles
evacuation
my blinking rate
my thinking rate
how fast I can wiggle my toes
or smell a rose
or swallow sweet wine
or chew an apple

This body is mine
second after second

GROOVES

My restless mind
paces
in grooves of security
and habit

I squeal to escape
and leap across the echoes of my mind
into the sky

DR. BENNER

Dr. Sandra Benner, a neurologist at the University of California, discovered something that was so strange, a peek into eternity, that she tried to hide it for fear it would expose God to destruction and exploitation for commercial and military purposes. She found a way to pray that worked, a way to align forces of the universe with one's desires. She used a combination of scientific instrumentation interfaced to the human mind, with a meditative, devotional attitude in which certain words were said and acts done that served as keys to open the locks to the cosmic forces.

The first experiments were conducted to explore the operation of the mind, and its ability to perform in a paranormal manner, for example to be clairvoyant. Experimentation was done on exceptional individuals, probing their brainwaves when they experienced paranormal activity. Certain brainwave patterns were associated with successful paranormal events.

Dr. Benner and her researchers learned that if they could train individuals to exhibit such brainwaves, then they were likely to demonstrate some paranormal activity. A way was discovered that allowed the scientists to train individuals to demonstrate the brainwave behavior associated with paranormal behavior. To their amazement, these individuals showed paranormal behavior. Then they started to study brainwaves during prayer. If this characteristic signature was present in the EEG during the prayer, the likelihood was greater that the prayer would be answered. Initially they used simple prayers, but they expanded to more complex prayers, and found, that their subjects remained successful if the EEG signature was present.

With some training, it was possible to train most individuals to tap into the infinite to have a very broad range of prayers answered. Within several years, the method was refined and developed and commercialized. Thousands underwent costly "cosmic orientation" or "achievement training" or "the opening." Many millionaires and billionaires appeared. Sales of expensive cars increased. Sophisticated electronic devices were developed that interfaced directly to the brain, and provided brainwave entrainment and feedback circuits with accelerated response. Higher frequency response was obtained. The military was active in this area, but dissatisfied that the full potential had not been achieved. The weak and uncontrollable link in the "creative" process was the human that had to think the prayer request. A collaboration of electrical engineers, pathologists, physiologists, neurologists and doctors from the National Institutes of Health and the Naval Hospital [and simultaneously in Budapest], attempted to use a human brain that was kept alive artificially in a controlled environment. After several unsuccessful attempts, the NIH group found a way to program the brain with the request, and to entrain the brain to perform as needed, displaying the proper brainwave patterns.

At the same time, a group of geneticists and molecular biologists at Harvard found a gene which when removed, produced rats that had EEG very similar to that observed by Dr. Benner.

The military developed a handheld device "the Armageddon" that contained a bath of cells and electronics. This device worked with 80% reliability. They wondered what the limits of its destructive power were; they conducted controlled tests in which they destroyed ever larger numbers of animals, buildings, and regions. They moved mountains. No limit to the power was detected. Devices were developed by the military that contained stored programs that represented destructive prayers, such as "create a fire that destroys all of Moscow and all its inhabitants." Great care was taken to insure that "Armageddon" were not used by nonmilitary personnel.

One day some hacker got a hold of one and programmed it to destroy the universe. Unfortunately, it worked. God decided she made a mistake in allowing a mechanism for God communication. Next universe, she decided, would be different.

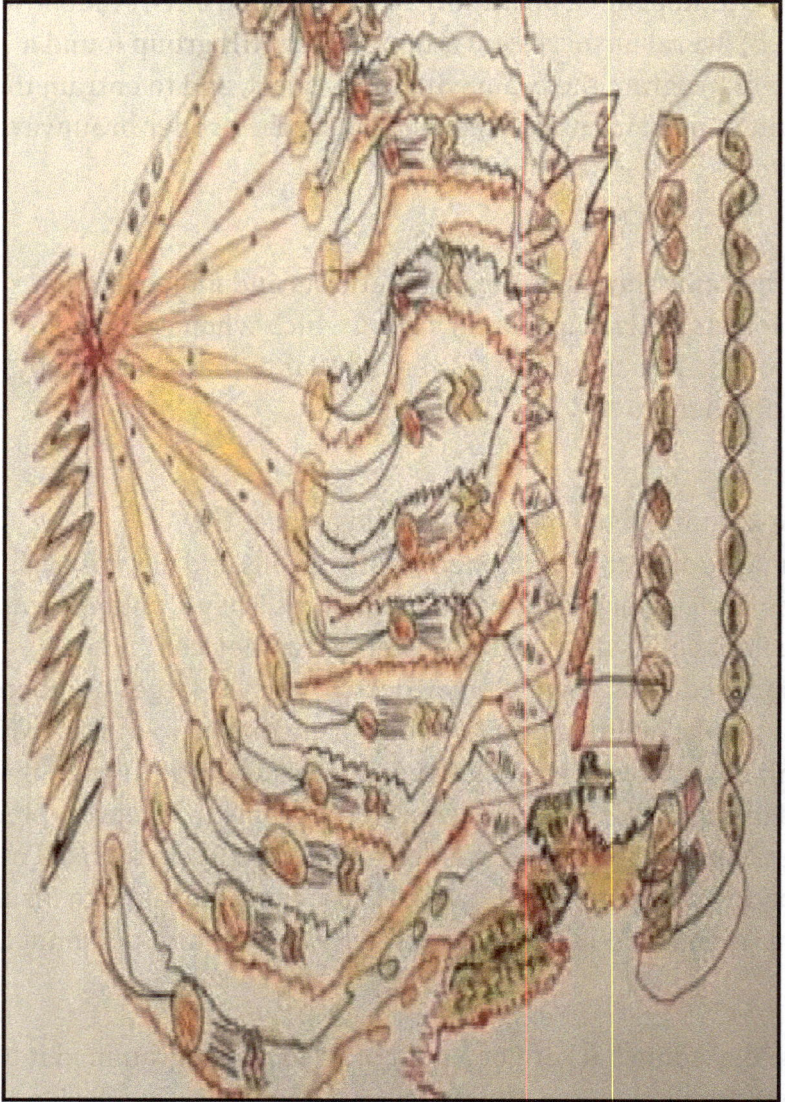

TAXES

I was worried about selling our house.
I dreamed I was walking down our beautiful staircase,
my hands firmly sliding along the banister
as I descended,
feeling the smoothness of the beautiful wood.

I woke at 5:15 AM so relieved and amused.
How could I worry about this when God, Christ,
and Guru are at the helm of the ship of my life?
It's like worrying about your taxes
when you have the greatest tax accountant in the world
working for you.

How can I worry about money
when divine principles say that
I should do my best today
and not worry about tomorrow.

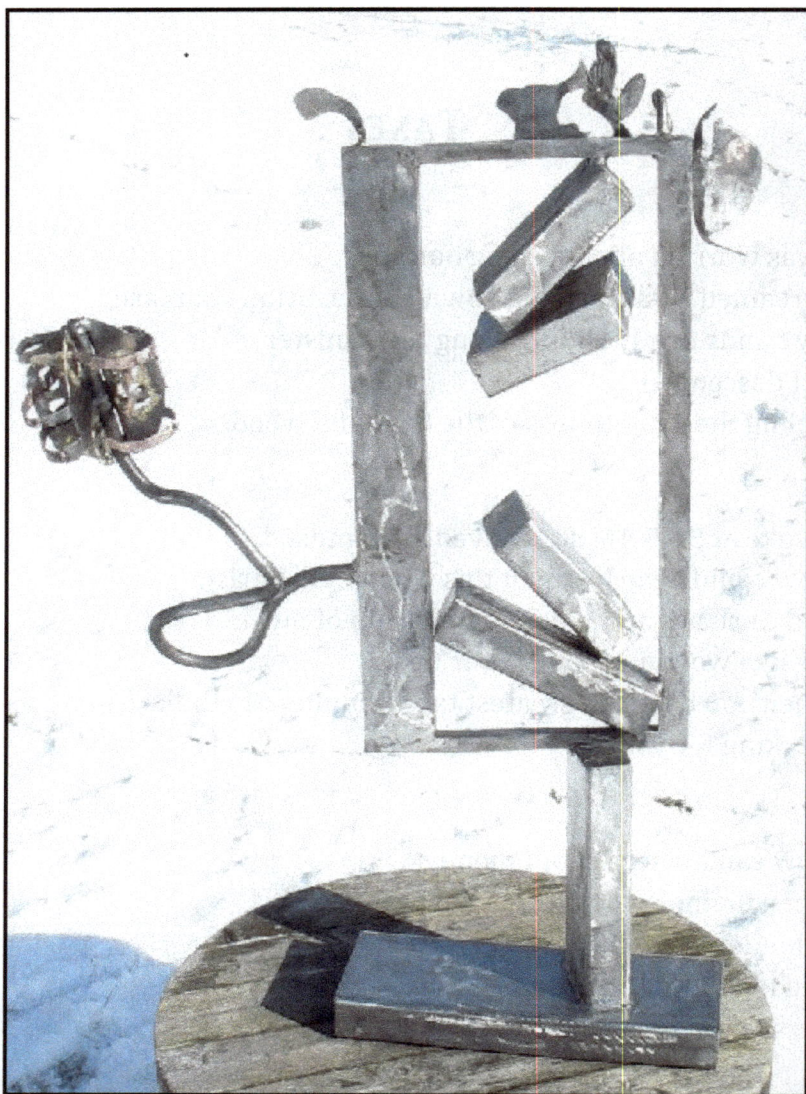

Tumbling Blocks - Welded steel 4' by 3'

PLANNING

My stomach reaches into my ears
wiggling, while
the clouds flow by
in stop motion,
and the newspaper is delivered to other people
and the generals in the 127 wars plan
how to kill better.
Meanwhile Pepsi plans to sell to the children in
Nicaragua,
Motorola strategizes to sell pagers to Poland
and phone systems to China, and
I sleep and dream and
wonder what to do with the gift of this body.
When Love knocks in my heart, this body will answer.

THE ONLY FEAR

In my mind, when love wakes
When the passion in me rises,
Like a turtle, I draw inward
Concealing my heart and freezing my hand.

What is this fear of myself?
This fear of acting on my feelings?

When swimming in the pond, I stay on the surface
I am afraid to let my feet go deep,
into the cold dark abyss of the unknown,
where dark monsters, muck, and seaweed
hide just below.

Is this the fear?
Is there only one fear?
Is there but one fear?

Darkness

DANCE OF SCIENCE

Twinkling stars
points of light
that travels
billions of years
to die in my eyes.

Nuclear furnaces of
unimaginable ferocity and size
making nuclei
bending space itself
filling the void.

And I am here
confused and wondering
why or how or what or when.

Scientists come and go
talking of
The Final Theory
The Emperor's New Strings
A proton is a cat's cradle
I am Jacob's Ladder.

One cell calls
in the darkness
demanding to be heard
like a beating heart.

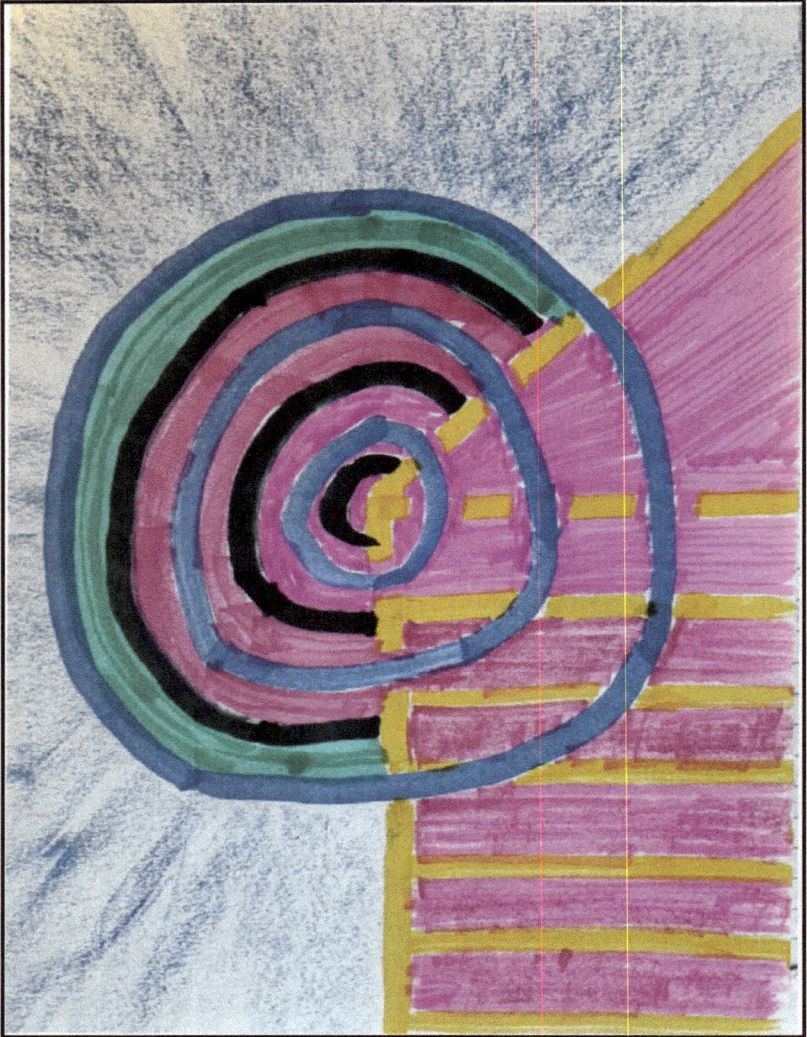

ENGINES OF TIME

Engines of time, lost
to the noise outside
racing across the corrugated islands of illusion:
a small peach bounced into a frog,
and I am finite and so on.

Tank cars crippled with viscous syrup
Old friends living in discarded crab shells
Birthday candles flaming, attended by a lieutenant
And other noises seducing my mind

Very Important   Memories lost in the dust of my attic
Very Important   Messages from my heart to myself
Carefully filed in a blue manila folder under M.

Glimmers of My truth
Lost in the piles of paper
Lost in the duties of my life
Waiting patiently, as their roots deepen,
to Bloom and Be Their Own,
To claim their infinite place.

Settling into being myself
Surrendering to being myself
Despite discomfort and disapproval

My heart pulsing
My breath flowing
I am alive.

MY WIFE IS ASLEEP

My wife is asleep.
Only my breathing
ripples the silence.
My eyes want to close
I want to see.
My mind wants to sleep
I want to think.
This is The Dance
between my Body and Me.

HOME THEATER STEREO

I built my stereo when I was a student many years ago.
I listen to it when I work in the basement.
When our son Colin was in Santiago, we used his stereo.
When he returned,
Mom gave Mary, my wife, a 69-dollar boombox for her
birthday
Two years ago.

Mary loves music. Her birthday is in 5 days.

Today I walked into a store to look.
Today I walked into a store and bought a home theater
stereo
for 3060.30 dollars,
without the rear speakers.

I am afraid.
When I left the store, I was lost. I sat in the parking lot
wondering where to go. I was hungry.
I turned left to go to go to Whole Foods.
I passed Toucheti's and turned right to go there.
Then I decided to go to Bakers Square.
I was lost, with no one inside to direct me.

I am afraid.
I wanted to buy the rear speakers but
I could not.
3060.30
no more.

Do I think I am made of gold?
Dare I act like I am made of gold?
Dare I tell the universe that I am a source of infinite
abundance?

ASK
Ask and it shall be answered unto you
Seek and you shall find
Knock and it shall be opened unto you.

Does this include a home theater stereo?
Can I walk on water?
Peter with his fear could not.
I ask for faith.
I will not put a basket over my candle.
Soon I will buy the rear speakers.
I hope my wife understands me.

The next morning, I am happy.
I own a beautiful new stereo.

LIGHT

Certain I will be disappointed
certain I will be busy
striving
and not arriving
in the foment of unfolding
in the devine metamorphosis
of a chrysalis.

Fumblings, bumblings
gropings, and mopings.
The elastic of time
bounces me against
rough sands, guides me divinely,
inexorably,
to crack my shell,
and release a crippled tortoise
into the blazing realization of light.

Keeping Busy

Left to wander the empty spaces of infinity, we are
like the psychotic who sees all
in a single dot in the Rorschach
must fill our senses to
hide the blinding sound of spirit
the light of life itself.

Hi Dumpy, hi Blitzd. Let's eat frog legs today while we
listen to records and wear perfume while the radio is
on that new channel with great call-in talking while
thinking about the time we sat on the bridge in the
rain, and our clothes got so wet we had to borrow
clothes that smelled so musty from the neighbors
running like a mad dog across the widest space he
could find saliva smeared on his lips and cheek like a
rose.

I eat oats as I think of my classes as I chew smelling
oranges and feel my legs on the edge of the seat deep
in the abyss of sensory wondering who I am and who
wrote this script.

SALT CAKES

A little time
the time of Being
like a bubble
misty in my eyes
is lost when I blink.

The fall so red
I never can remember its beauty.
Why is that?

Did I do all this? I?
Or did You? or They?
Or all these Other People?
Was it my mother or yours?

Do I dare to eat my liver?
Do I dare to pick my nose?
Do I dare to jump into the ocean?

I had a dog whose name was Matthew.
He never complained. He loved to play.
He loved to eat and to sleep with me.

80

He never talked, but always listened
and accepted me. He must have loved me very much.

But that was before TV and automatic popcorn makers,
when instrument panels had round gauges and white
lights and you wore your golden hair combed.

The spider on the kitchen floor is so ignorant
of the parlor. She doesn't recognize the giant god I am.
Why is that?

WHAT MONA, AGE 4, EXPLAINED TO ME

If you don't like what you do, spank your mind.

(Said by a girl who was never spanked!)

MY FEARLESS HERO

We all have heroes we admire.
Boris, our huskie, was my teacher.
Like many great teachers, he never explained himself.
One had to watch to obtain the lesson.

When he was hungry, if there was anything
to put in his mouth and chew,
he ate.
It didn't bother him to eat the rejected
or unpleasant parts,
the eyes or guts or gristle, fur or feet.
With great care and patience,
he would enjoy eating
inexorably
a turtle shell or a raccoon leg,
living in the moment of each chew.

Boris would walk into the pond
unconcerned with the black muck his feet
would sink into, or any reptiles he might disturb.
He would stand in the hot sun,
enjoying his moments in the cool water.

In the middle of the night,
he would go outside, into the fields and woods,
barefooted, naked, without a flashlight,
into the prickly ash, the nettles, the blackberries,
the coyotes, smelling whatever he smelled,
enjoying his moments of exploration.

Boris would put his nose anywhere,
lick anything with his huge tongue,
walk anywhere he wanted,
chase anything he wanted.

It may surprise you but
he never got hurt,
although he did get skunked a few times,
and when he was tired
he slept soundly.

THE DAY BORIS DIED

On Thursday, Boris our huskie
didn't come home at night.
He was quite sick and I
thought it might be his time.

Next morning I found him sitting on his butt
in the cold water at the edge of our pond,
to ease his pain,
with his body covered up to his shoulders,
in one of the most beautiful spots on our farm.

I sat with him,
and took the water in my hands
and put it all over his back and face,
bathing him,
gently crying the tears of a noble lover
knowing the end is near.

I told him I was sorry about all my shortcomings,
that I had failed to groom him more.
He used to love to be groomed,
to lie there like a king
being groomed.

I thought,
laughing and crying,
what more could he have done,
with his coat filled with copious samples of everything
that lived in the woods,
to ask for grooming.

I could see, that I could have done better,
but I did not feel bad about it,
it was more an observation.

I told him I loved him
and I know he knew what I was saying.
He accepted my love
as he accepted his life.

I put more water on him and baptized him
with the divine love in me,
and thought such a noble dog
must surely
go to a beautiful place after death.

What Is Your Programming?

I notice from observing myself that I am a machine programmed to work, like a bee or a squirrel, exchanging services for things, which I accumulate, until I am too tired or old to continue accumulating. An electrochemical nerve impulse travels along a linear collection of special cells, and I move. Who is running this sophisticated mission-oriented system, and what is the mission? Who controls the chemistry? I have not been programmed to think about why I am busy as a bee, or what I am really doing.

At dawn I see the sun through my window and feel the miracle of rebirth. A few minutes of peace and gratitude pass, and I think about what I should be doing that day. Doing things that need to be done, not frivolous things.

Birds are birds all day and night, and they sing and eat and fly as birds do. Perhaps I could teach them to read, and open them up to greater experiences, saving them from their biological programming and destiny. Or even better, perhaps that cardinal could teach me to sing and eat sunflower seeds and fly.

WHEN WHAT IS MOST PRECIOUS IS LOST

Reaching into the black cool waters
With a gentle probing touch, hoping to not get soiled,
First my fingers, then my hand slowly disappears.
I breath once, and my elbow is gone.

The black dread extends far beyond my simple reach.
My hand probes gently, tentatively, furtively,
Discovering strange substances,
And still no signal is given.

Lowering my head towards the water
I see myself and my destiny reflected.
Surrendering for a moment,
I disappear into the black water.

I try to reorganize myself and realize
With unexpected pleasure
I have shed my skin like a giant snake.
I have grown long pointed teeth in a fierce jaw.
I am the monster of the deep,
The monster I had always feared.

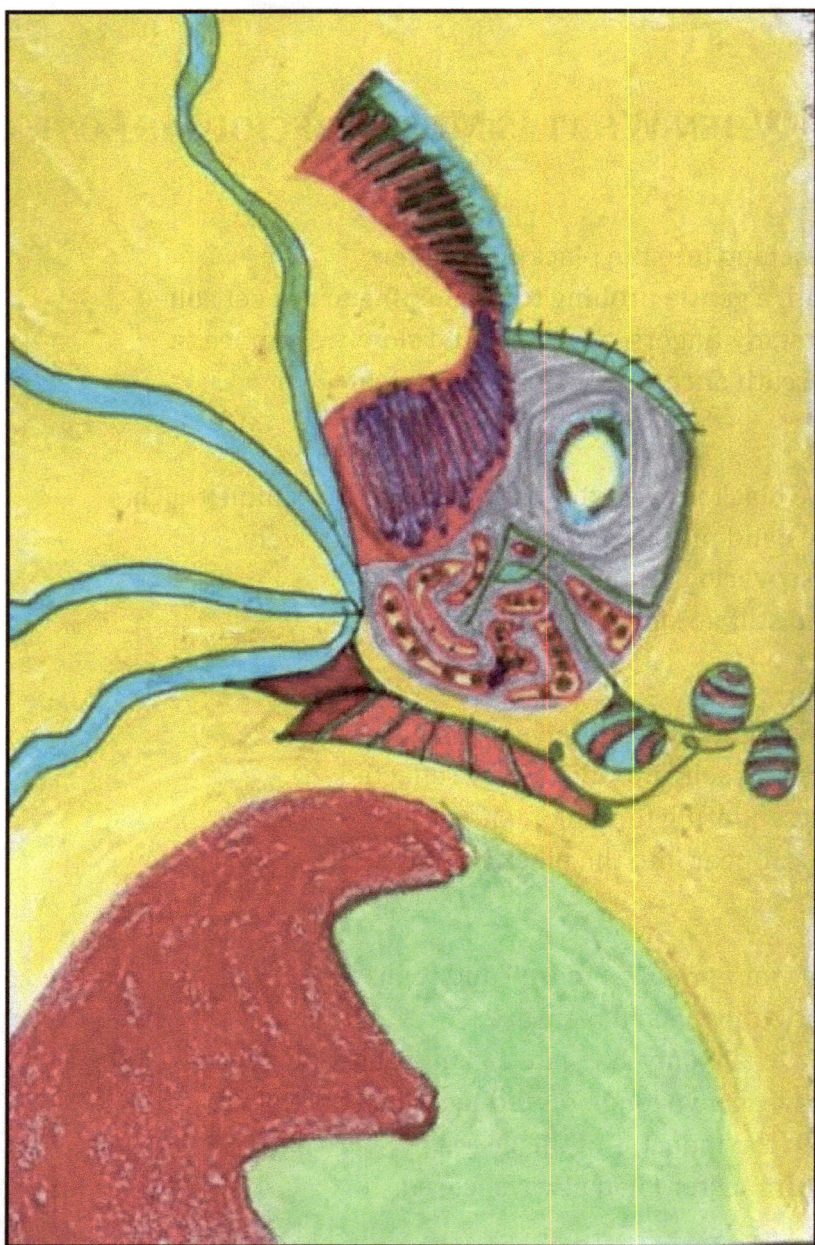

Transformations

Sometimes I like to sleep.
I lie down, and enjoy the peace and relaxation
of my body on soft sheets.
This is the time of communion with the divine.
I am so blessed that I can sleep when I want.
I remember as a college student,
having to wake up after a five-minute nap.
The positive effect of eternity,
all wrapped into a small piece of soft bread
that can be moved into a bread bowl,
defying all of the baking principles known to man.

Once, when I was young,
I remember the joy of eating a popsicle
watching it melt in the warm sun,
dripping down the handle onto my hand,
licking my fingers, licking the popsicle, licking the sky.
All forces immortalized in a frozen orange object.

And once in a great while, the blessings of
multi-floral amplitudes of Fourier transforms
would transform my beliefs into a kind of knowledge.

And now I can tell the story of my life.
I was born, lived for many years, and passed away.
All too brief. Is this the last chapter in the Cosmic book?

Now, I can say to you that I am here and you are there.
This is why we have to stretch our minds
across the rubber bands of space.
Now, is the time for us to love ourselves
and love our brothers and sisters.
Now is the time to release the secret deep-seated affection
that we have within our hearts for each other.

EPILOGUE

My poems
Reveal my self
My treasured neurotic ruminations
My carefully constructed
Inferiority complex
My insights
My mind at work.

Meanwhile my spirit
Watches
Amused at all my gyrations,
Offers illumination,
Quietly loving me.

Earlier Work from 1975

Steel, sisal rope, leather, and brass wire, 8' x 3'

Welded steel and sisal rope, 6' x 4'

ABOUT THE AUTHOR

This is the first time G. Jordan Maclay has published some of his poems, art and sculpture. He is a quantum physicist who has done seminal research in quantum energy and microsensors for four decades. His lifelong interest in art, psychology, philosophy, and spirituality informs this book.

He has published over 80 professional scientific journal papers and has 15 patents. He received his PhD from Yale in 1972, was a post-doctoral researcher at Argonne National Laboratory. He worked for two years as a welder, so he could learn how to make welded steel sculpture, taught elementary and middle school, did new product development, and then taught and did research at University of Illinois at Chicago for two decades.

After an early retirement from UIC, he moved to the Wisconsin countryside with his wife and two young children, and founded Quantum Fields LLC, where he has been Chief Scientist for the last 25 years. He has an older son from a previous marriage who lives in California. He enjoyed creating these poems and art while living in Wisconsin. He currently lives in Illinois.

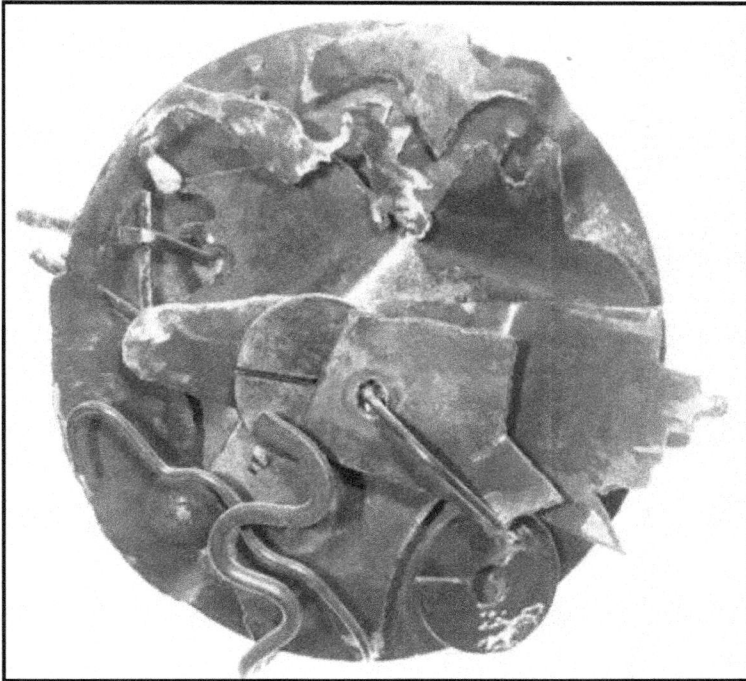

Welded Steel 20" diameter by 12 "

www.ingramcontent.com/pod-product-compliance
Lightning Source LLC
Chambersburg PA
CBHW060117050426
42448CB00010B/1908